BUZZIN' TONIGHT

The Drones perform their parts with a bee-like wr
bottom and flapping of the arms.

BEE	*1.*	I'm a busy little body,
		'Cos I'm gonna have a party tonight.
DRONES		*Buzz-buzz, buzzin' tonight.*
BEE		I'm a busy little body,
		'Cos I'm gonna have a party tonight.
DRONES		*Buzz-buzz, buzzin' tonight.*
BEE		The hostess with the mostest, the brightest and best,
		All done up in a stripy vest.
		So come along and be my guest
		At the party tonight.
DRONES		*Buzz-buzz, buzzin' tonight.*
BEE	*2.*	I'm a busy little body,
		'Cos I'm gonna have a party tonight.
DRONES		*Buzz-buzz, buzzin' tonight.*
BEE		I'm a busy little body,
		'Cos I'm gonna have a party tonight.
DRONES		*Buzz-buzz, buzzin' tonight.*
BEE		There's wining and there's dining, the finest and best.
		Some are trying to eat up the rest.
		So come along and be my guest
		At the party tonight.
DRONES		*Buzz-buzz, buzzin' tonight.*

Bee dances during REFRAIN

DRONES	*REFRAIN*	*B, B, B, B, Buzz-buzz, buzzin' tonight.*
and BEE		*B, B, B, B, Buzz-buzz, buzzin' tonight.*
		B, B, B, B, Buzz-buzz, buzzin' tonight.
		B, B, B, B, Buzz-buzz, buzzin' tonight.
		So come along and be my guest
		At the party tonight. Buzzin' tonight.
(whispered)		*YEH!*

Drones retire to tableau position. Bumble Bee perches on a flower and acts as hostess of the fiesta, welcoming with enthusiasm each new minibeast as they arrive.

Fact: Bumble bees are social insects and live in communities.

A flamboyant Cicada and his band of Crickets with percussion instruments enter with a flourish, gathering to form a dance band.

BEE

Here comes the leader of the band,
Conductor's baton in his hand . . .
Señor Cicada starts his song,
And all the Crickets play along.

Señor Cicada conducts the band.

Song 2   # CICADA SERENADE

ALL   *1.*

**When the Cicada played a serenade
He made a sound
So intoxicating,
They came from miles around,
Dancing and swaying
To the rhythm of the band.
It was the best fiesta in the land.**

REFRAIN

**Si, si, si, si, si,
The Cicada played a song.
Ch, ch, ch, ch, ch,
Chirped the Crickets all night long.**

Enter Firefly dancing

2.

**And when the Firefly darted in the sky
It was a sight
So very hypnotising,
It brightened up the night,
Dancing and swaying
To the rhythm of the band.
It was the best fiesta in the land.**

REFRAIN
(in English)

**Si, si, si, si, si,
The Cicada played a song.
Ch, ch, ch, ch, ch,
Chirped the Crickets all night long.**

ALTERNATIVE REFRAIN
(in Spanish)

**Si, si, si, si, si,
La cigarra canta el son.
Ch, ch, ch, ch, ch,
La, la, la misma canción.**

**Fact: The cicada makes a persistent sound by a movement of its abdomen.
The cricket makes a chirping by rubbing its hind legs together.**

4

Minibeast Madness!

by Debbie Campbell
edited by Alison Hedger

A fun look into the lives of minibeasts on midsummer's night
for performance any time of the year

PUPIL'S BOOK
Contains the play and song words

The Teacher's Book, Order No. GA11090, contains the piano score,
vocal lines, chord symbols, optional percussion parts and production notes.

A matching tape cassette of the music for rehearsals and performances is also available,
Order No. GA11092, Side A with vocals included and Side B with vocals omitted.

© Copyright 1999 Golden Apple Productions
A division of Chester Music Limited
8/9 Frith Street, London W1V 5TZ

Pupil's Book Order No. GA11091

ISBN 0-7119-7566-3

SCENE – In a Garden

OPENING MUSIC

Enter Fly/Flies-on-a-wall who address audience and sit on a wall.
Divide the narration as appropriate.

FLY

Hi!
I'm a kind of common fly
Who likes to watch the world go by.
And as I hover silently
You'd be amazed at what I see.

In a wild and woody place I know
Where not a lot of people go,
The creepy-crawlies come to play
And dance midsummer's night away.

Since time began each generation
Has a special invitation
To hop in, drop in, creep and crawl –
Like guests arriving at a ball.

And though they may look odd to you,
I'll introduce you to a few.
So come along and join the fun.
The best fiesta has begun.

Enter Bumble Bee and Drones who gather around the flowers.

FLY

The hostess is a bumble bee.
She greets her guests excitedly.
And every creature has a chance
To sing a song and do a dance.

Fact: Flies have compound eyes. All the better for seeing with.

Repeat Verse 1. **When the Cicada played a serenade**
He made a sound
So intoxicating,
They came from miles around,
Dancing and swaying
To the rhythm of the band.
It was the best fiesta in the land.

Coda **It was the best fiesta in the land.**
It was the best fiesta . . . in the land.

(Spoken) **Olé!**

FLY   Now the party has begun
And everyone is having fun.
But they're so busy, they don't see
The gang of three behind the tree.

Enter Inspector Secticide and his Bug Squad – emerging from behind the especially large tree where they have been hiding.

BUG SQUAD   We're the Bug Squad. We're the best
At finding all those little pests
That creep and crawl. We get them all.
And one by one we watch them fall.

INSPECTOR S.   I'm Inspector Secticide,
And in my work I take a pride.
This is Snitch and this is Swat.
Together we're a clever lot.

Snitch and Swat proudly produce a violin case of weapons.

SNITCH   This ordinary violin case
Converts into a hiding place.
Secretly concealed in here
Is all our insect-fighting gear.

Snitch takes out the weapons one by one and shows them to the audience.

SNITCH   A magnifying glass to spot 'em.
SWAT   A fly-swatter with which to swat 'em.
SNITCH   An ear trumpet so we can hear 'em.
SWAT   A loud hailer to shout and scare 'em.
SNITCH   A net to catch 'em and upset 'em.
SWAT   And finally a spray to get 'em.
SNITCH/SWAT   The case is closed!

Violin case is slammed shut.
Inspector Secticide finds a spider's web (stage left) and examines it with the spy glass.

INSPECTOR S.　　　　　　Come on, use your common sense
　　　　　　　　　　　　　　For here's a thread of evidence.
　　　　　　　　　　　　　　I spy with my glass eye
　　　　　　　　　　　　　　A spider's web and one dead fly.

Inspector Secticide and Bug Squad mime getting entangled in the web as it "unravels".

FLY　　　　　　　　　　　They try unravelling the thread
　　　　　　　　　　　　　　But get all tangled up instead.
　　　　　　　　　　　　　　A dizzy spider then descends
　　　　　　　　　　　　　　And hurries off to join her friends.

Daisy the Tipsy Spider "descends", tottering and trying to keep her balance, obviously the worse for a drink or two.

BEE　　　　　　　　　　　Here she comes all hail and hearty
　　　　　　　　　　　　　　The life and soul of every party.
　　　　　　　　　　　　　　So let us have a big hand please
　　　　　　　　　　　　　　For Daisy on her high trapeze.

Enter the other trapeze-act spiders who perform a routine during the next song. Daisy "walks" the tightrope and "swings" on a trapeze. At appropriate moments she wobbles but just manages to keep her balance, ending with a dramatic final fall.

Song 3　　　　　# DAISY THE TIPSY SPIDER

ALL　　　　　　　*1.*　　**Daisy the tipsy spider**
　　　　　　　　　　　　　Is fond of a bottle of cider.
　　　　　　　　　　　　　The cider is fizzy and after a bubble
　　　　　　　　　　　　　Old Daisy is dizzy and starts seeing double and . . .

　　　　　　REFRAIN　　**Whoopsidazy, Daisy!**
　　　　　　　　　　　　　Her drinking is driving us crazy.
　　　　　　　　　　　　　See her reel on the ceiling and crawl up the wall.
　　　　　　　　　　　　　Oh! One of these days poor old Daisy will fall.

　　　　　　　　　　2.　**Daisy the tipsy spider**
　　　　　　　　　　　　　Is fond of a bottle of cider.
　　　　　　　　　　　　　High as a kite on a tightrope thread,
　　　　　　　　　　　　　The cider inside her goes right to her head and then . . .

　　　　　　REFRAIN　　**Whoopsidazy, Daisy!**
　　　　　　　　　　　　　Her drinking is driving us crazy.　　　⎫
　　　　　　　　　　　　　See her reel on the ceiling and crawl up the wall.　⎬ *twice*
　　　　　　　　　　　　　Oh! One of these days poor old Daisy will . . .　⎭
　　　　　　　　　　　　　Fall.

The spiders move to tableau position.

Fact: Spiders spin webs to catch flies. Then they suck out the liquid from the flies' bodies.

Inspector Secticide notices the large dung-coloured cushion.

INSPECTOR S.	It's very muddy up ahead So just be careful where you tread. (*Snitch falls in mud*)
SWAT	Look out Snitch, you clumsy twit Trust you, to put your foot in it.
FLY	But as he sinks down in the goo He pulls the others in it too. (*Inspector and Swat fall into mud*) The dung beetles then seize their chance And hurry off to join the dance.

Enter Dung Beetles in animated mood, emerging from behind the large dung-coloured cushion.

BEE	In ancient Egypt they were holy. Scarabs now are rather lowly. Wherever there is muck you'll find The dung beetles not far behind.

Fly points to Dung Beetles and holds his/her nose!

Song 4 **DUNG BEETLE BOOGIE**

(The first REFRAIN and the verses are sung by the Dung Beetles – it may be appropriate to give some solo parts)

REFRAIN (*digging*) (*points to audience*) (*digging*)	**I'm a Dung Beetle,** **But let me tell you people** **Ain't nothin' wrong with diggin' dung** **If you're a Dung Beetle.**
(*twisting down*) 1. (*twisting back up*) (*rubbing tummy*)	**Born and raised, spent all my days** **Down among the dung,** **Just havin' fun.** **Love it by the ton, I dig it.**
REFRAIN **ALL:**	**I'm a Dung Beetle . . .**
2. (*lying down on back* *waving arms & legs in the air*)	**When I'm done with diggin' dung** **And my time has come to rest,** **I'm gonna lay me** **In the place I love the best. You guessed it.** (*jumping up*)
REFRAIN **ALL:** (*digging*) (*spoken*)	**I'm a Dung Beetle,** **But let me tell you people** **Ain't nothin' wrong with diggin' dung** **If you're a dung-digger, dung-digger,** **Dung-digger, dung-digger,** **Dung-digger son of a gun.** **I just dig that dung!** (*rubbing tummy*)

The Dung Beetles move to tableau position.

Fact: Dung beetles help each other to roll large balls of dung which they then bury, and lay their eggs inside.

INSPECTOR S.	In this business I have learned
	You never leave a stone unturned. (*approaches boulder*)
SNITCH	I bet that underneath we'll see
	A creepy-crawly colony.

Bug Squad make tremendous effort to roll boulder. As boulder "moves" the Silly Millipede appears from behind, waves a cheery hello and nimbly trips to centre stage, ready for next song.

FLY	They try to lift the heavy stone
	Then drop it with a painful groan.
	A millipede bids them good day
	Then makes a nimble getaway.
BEE	It is a funny sight indeed
	To watch the Silly Millipede.
	For as she starts to sway and dance
	She sends herself into a trance.

Song 5 — THE SILLY MILLIPEDE

With an Eastern-inspired dance with smooth swaying body rhythms and hypnotic arm gestures.

ALL	**Ask any Silly Millipede**
	How many legs she needs to speed
	Along the ground, around the floor.
	She's bound to say she's not quite sure.
	For she can only count to ten,
	And then she has to start again.
REFRAIN	**One two three four five six seven eight nine ten,**
	Then she must start again.
	Centipedes plenty count up to twenty.
	Millipedes only ten.
	See she is coming.
	Pitter patter all her legs are running.
	Millipede is very shy and quickly she will hurry by,
	Then in the twinkle of an eye she's gone.
	Ask any Silly Millipede
	How many legs she needs to speed
	Along the ground, around the floor.
	She's bound to say she's not quite sure.
	For she can only count to ten,
	And then she has to start again.
REFRAIN	**One two three four five six seven eight nine ten,**
	Then she must start again.
	Centipedes plenty count up to twenty.
	Millipedes only ten.

Fact: Millipede means 'thousand feet' but in fact millipedes have at most 180 legs.

Millipede moves away from centre stage. Inspector Secticide beckons to the Bug Squad as he discovers the trail left by Snail.

INSPECTOR S.
Come and see what I have found,
A silver line along the ground.
You can bet this shiny trail
Will lead us to a slimy snail.

FLY
They find a shell, but then decide
There isn't anything inside.
But after they have gone away
The snail inside comes out to play.

Snail cheekily pops his head out of the shell, smiling. Then stares in glum mood at other insects some of whom are flitting about.

BEE
The Snail can only stand and stare
At flighty insects in the air.
She'd love to dance and fly as well
But cannot come out of her shell.

Song 6   SNAIL HOUSE BLUES

Enter rest of snails and lie on stomachs with heads facing audience and chins resting on hands looking fed up.

SNAIL(S)   *REFRAIN*
**I've got the snail house blues.
But tell me what can I do?
I wanna choose where I live,
And live where I choose.
I've got the snail house blues.**
(last time only) **Oh yeh.**

     1.
**Wish I didn't have to wear
This armour-plated gear.** *(pointing to "shell" hat)*
(running movement with arms) **I wanna run, and have some fun,**
(throw arms in air) **And throw myself in the air.**

     REFRAIN
I've got the snail house blues . . .

     2.
**They may say because I'm slow
I'm just a layabout.
But can't they tell inside this shell**
(punch air with fists) **Is a tearaway trying to get out?**

     REFRAIN
I've got the snail house blues . . .

Oh yeh.

> **Fact: Snails need to eat a lot of calcium to form their shell.**

All snails slowly move away from centre stage as Mr and Mrs Mantis enter, arm-in-arm, full of smiles.

INSPECTOR S.

Hello, hello. What have we here?
Looks like a very funny pair.
Let's follow them without their knowing
Then we'll find out where they're going.

FLY

The Praying Mantis and his mate
Are late for their important date.
And in their hurry they don't see
The Bug Squad lurking by the tree.

BEE

A party wouldn't be complete
Without a special treat to eat–
But Mr Praying Mantis do
Be careful, or it could be you.

Song 7

PRAYING MANTIS PRAYER

Mr and Mrs Manis enter arm-in-arm, walk slowly along an aisle during hymn. Throughout song Mrs Mantis seems over-eager to have Mr Mantis all to herself.

ALL
(solemnly)
1.
**Say a prayer for the Praying Mantis
As he prepares to meet his mate.
How will she treat him? Maybe she'll eat him!
What is his future? What is his fate?**

MR MANTIS *REFRAIN*
(gospel-like off beat clapping)
**Oh Lord, up above
Here in the arms of the one I love.
Oh Lord in the sky, am I gonna live or die?
Everybody sing**

ALL *REFRAIN*
**Oh Lord, up above
Here in the arms of the one I love.
Oh Lord in the sky, am I gonna live or die?**

ALL
2.
**O, Mantis Religiosa
Varium semper femina.
Aut amat, aut odit
Vade in pace, amica.**

There is a tense moment as Mrs Mantis makes her decision either to gobble Mr Mantis up, or let him go. They move away from centre stage.

Fact: The female praying mantis, depending on her mood, sometimes will eat the male after mating.

Inspector Secticide opens violin case, removes insecticide spray, holds it aloft and gives it a mighty shake and replaces it inside violin case, leaving the lid open.

INSPECTOR S.	Now it's time for us to fix Our tasty little cocktail mix. Shake it well, and then replace Back inside the violin case.
FLY	High up in the evening sky (*enter Madam Butterfly*) The Butterfly comes fluttering by. Little does this creature know What they are plotting down below.

Baby Caterpillars enter and snuggle down together.

BEE	The Caterpillar sleepy-heads Are snuggled in their cosy beds. Now lovely Madam Butterfly Will sing a gentle lullaby.

Song 8   CATERPILLAR LULLABY

BUTTERFLY	*1.*	**Hushaby, the wind will sigh** **A caterpillar lullaby.** **Cradled in cocoon you lie.** **Soon it will shake you, gently awake you,** **Then you'll be a pretty butterfly.**
ALL	*REFRAIN*	**Pretty butterfly, pretty butterfly.** **Pretty butterfly, pretty butterfly.**
BUTTERFLY	*2.*	**'Doucement' dit le vent,** **'Doucement chenille enfant.** **Couché en cocon tu dors.** **Il te secouera, pour te reveiller,** **Puis tu seras joli papillon.'**
ALL	*REFRAIN*	**Joli papillon, joli papillon.** **Joli papillon, joli papillon.**

Fact: Unlike 'Madam Butterfly', the butterfly leaves its eggs to fend for themselves once she has laid them.

The Bug Squad approach Madam Butterfly and Sergeant Swat takes the insecticide spray and aims it menacingly at the minibeasts. Other "weapons" are taken by the Squad and held in a threatening manner.

INSPECTOR S.
(*shouting through hailer*)
SWAT

Stop the music. Stop the dance!
Your time is up. You've had your chance. (*Minibeasts hold up hands*)
Stay where you are. Don't try to run.
The **pest** fiesta has begun.

FLY

The Bumble Bee sounds the alarm.
She knows they've come to do them harm.
And then the Bug Squad starts to spray
The minibeasts who turn away. (*turn backs to audience & Bug Squad*)

BEE

Who are these strangers that I see?
They do not look like guests to me.
What do they want? Why are they here?
They've come to get us all I fear.

Song 9

MARCH OF THE MINIBEASTS

BUG SQUAD
whispering

1.
**We'll seek 'em and find 'em,
We'll creep up behind 'em,
We'll give 'em a bit of a SCARE!** (*clap*)
**We'll spray 'em and swat 'em.
They won't know what's got 'em.
We'll show 'em who's boss around here.**

MINIBEASTS *REFRAIN*
(*facing away from audience and marching on spot*)

There's nowhere to run and there's nowhere to hide
(*extend right then left hands*)
From the powers of Inspector Secticide.
(*shielding face with hands*)
Now the time is right, we must all unite,
(*hold up right then left fists*)
And send him on his way tonight.
(*shake fists in air*)

ALL MINIBEASTS
(*turn to audience*)

2.
**We'll get up their noses and tickle their toeses,
We'll give 'em a bit of a FRIGHT!** (*clap*)
**We'll sting 'em and fight 'em.
We'll bug 'em and bite 'em,
And show them what's wrong and what's right.**

MINIBEASTS *REFRAIN*
(*march on spot confidently*)

**There's nowhere to run and there's nowhere to hide
From the powers of Inspector Secticide.
Now the time is right, we must all unite,
And send him on his way tonight.**

12

ALL	*3.*	All the creepy crawly beetles and the bees And the flies and the fleas, All the incy-wincy spiders and the slugs And the snails and the bugs. Side by side they stood that night In the shining light of the firefly bright. Some were shivering, some were lame, But all the Minibeasts said the same.
ALL	*REFRAIN*	There's nowhere to run and there's nowhere to hide From the powers of Inspector Secticide. Now the time is right, we must all unite, And send him on his way tonight.
	(shouted)	**TONIGHT!**

The terrified Bug Squad are pursued by the triumphant minibeasts.

Straight into next song.

Song 10   # I'VE GOT A BEE IN MY BONNET

INSPECTOR S.	*(shouted)*	**YAROO!**	
	1.	I've got a bee in my bonnet,	*(holding head)*
		I've got bugs in my bed.	*(hugging body)*
		I've got a weird kinda buzzin' Goin' on in my head.	*(point to head, circular motion)*
		And I've got ants in my pants	*(one hand on behind)*
		And a flea in my ear.	*(other hand points to ear)*
		I've gotta get out of here.	*(walk on spot)*
BUG SQUAD	*REFRAIN*	Goodbye, cheerio,	*(waving)*
		So long, we gotta go. This time I know for sure We're not coming back no more.	
ALL		**YIPPEE!**	
	2.	You've got a bee in your bonnet, You've got bugs in your bed. You've got a weird kinda buzzin' Goin' on in your head. And you've got ants in your pants And a flea in your ear. You've gotta get out. You've gotta get out. You've gotta get out of here.	

Exit Inspector Secticide and his Bug Squad.

FLY
At last the enemy has gone,
So let the fiesta carry on,
Strike up the band, now let's begin –
And everybody, (*points to audience*) please join in!

Señor Cicada starts up the band, and the festivities continue.

Reprise Song 2   CICADA SERENADE

Inspector Secticide and his Bug Squad return and also join in the party!

ALL
1.   When the Cicada played a serenade
He made a sound
So intoxicating,
They came from miles around,
Dancing and swaying
To the rhythm of the band.
It was the best fiesta in the land.

REFRAIN
Si, si, si, si, si,
The Cicada played a song.
Ch, ch, ch, ch, ch,
Chirped the Crickets all night long.

2.   And when the Firefly darted in the sky
It was a sight
So very hypnotising,
It brightened up the night,
Dancing and swaying
To the rhythm of the band.
It was the best fiesta in the land.

REFRAIN
(in English)
Si, si, si, si, si,
The Cicada played a song.
Ch, ch, ch, ch, ch,
Chirped the Crickets all night long.

ALTERNATIVE REFRAIN
(in Spanish)
Si, si, si, si, si,
La cigarra canta el son.
Ch, ch, ch, ch, ch,
La, la, la misma cancíon.

Repeat Verse 1.   **When the Cicada played a serenade**
He made a sound
So intoxicating,
They came from miles around,
Dancing and swaying
To the rhythm of the band.
It was the best fiesta in the land.

Coda   **It was the best fiesta in the land.**
It was the best fiesta . . . in the land.

(Shouted)   **Olé!**

THE END

15

Other musicals by Debbie Campbell

AVAILABLE FROM GOLDEN APPLE PRODUCTIONS

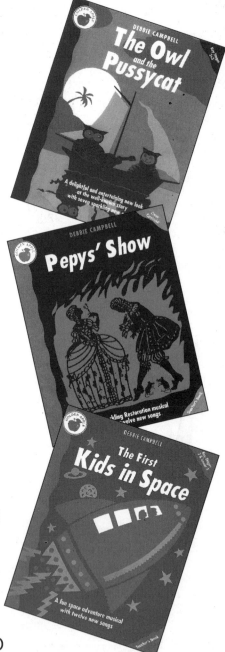

The Owl And The Pussycat

(8-14yrs)

A comical account of what really happened when the Owl and the Pussycat went to sea...
Suitable as a musical or concert piece, this is a fresh look at the well-known story by Edward Lear, with nine great new songs.

Teacher's book GA11066
Pupil's Book GA11067
Cassette GA11068

Pepys' Show

(8-13yrs)

With 12 lively new songs, dance and drama, this Restoration musical brings alive the hardships felt during the time of the Bubonic Plague and the Great Fire of London.

Teacher's Book GA11050
Pupil's Book GA11051
Cassette GA11052

The First Kids In Space

(8-14yrs)

A fun space adventure musical, full of information on technology and the solar system. Set in the year 2020 and featuring space cadets, a friendly robot, riotous androids and the planets of the solar system!

Teacher's Book GA11013
Pupil's Book GA11014
Cassette GA11015

AVAILABLE FROM NOVELLO

The Bumblesnouts Save The World
Visitors from outer space highlight the importance of caring for our environment in this funny and lively musical
NOV070507

Big Momma
The story of a baby elephant's journey from the wild to captivity in a zoo, told through 10 moving songs.
NOV070508

The Emerald Crown
A fresh look at the rainforest, told by the animals: featuring the rapping Toucan and the 'Amazon Aristocrat' Jaguar.
NOV070519

Ocean Commotion
Hear the Barnacles singing the blues with this unmissable musical set deep in the ocean.
NOV072168

ISBN 0-7119-7566-3

9 780711 975668

Golden Apple Productions
A division of Chester Music Limited
Exclusive distributors:
Music Sales Limited, Newmarket Road, Bury St. Edmunds, Suffolk IP33 3YB

Pupil's Book Order No. GA11091